TRUE STORIES OF

Animal Tricks and Talents

BY ARNOLD RINGSTAD

The Child's World

Published by The Child's World®
1980 Lookout Drive • Mankato, MN 56003-1705
800-599-READ • www.childsworld.com

Acknowledgments
The Child's World®: Mary Berendes, Publishing Director
Red Line Editorial: Editorial direction
The Design Lab: Design
Amnet: Production

Photographs © Austral Int/Rex Features/AP Images, cover
(center), 1, 7; Gareth Fuller/EMPPL PA Wire/AP Images,
back cover (left), 5; PhotoDisc, cover (right), 1, 3 (bottom), 14;
Shutterstock Images, cover (top), 1, 2–3 , 23; Comstock/
Thinkstock, back cover (right), 3 (top), 18; Thinkstock, back
cover (bottom), 8; Don Campbell/The Herald-Palladium/AP
Images, 4, 19; Richard Austin/Rex Features/AP Images, 9; Rex
Features/AP Images, 10, 15; Nancy Chan/Six Flags Discovery
Kingdom/AP Images, 12; Edward Westmacott/Thinkstock, 13;
Rex Features/AP Images, 15; Ivan Sekretarev/AP Images, 16;
Anatolii Tsekhmister/Thinkstock, 17; The Gorilla Foundation/AP
Images, 21

ISBN 9781626873605
LCCN 2014930699

Printed in the United States of America
Mankato, MN
July, 2014
PA02225

ABOUT THE AUTHOR

*Arnold Ringstad lives in
Minnesota. His cat is talented
at sleeping for many hours at
a time.*

CONTENTS

ANIMAL TRICKS AND TALENTS

Pet dogs do simple tricks all the time. Many dogs sit, bark, or shake hands. But some animals can do amazing tricks. Playing piano, painting, and water-skiing are just a few examples. Read on to learn about these and other stories of animal tricks and talents.

This squirrel isn't the only animal with an amazing talent.

Walking Like a Person

Humans are the only **primates** that normally walk on two legs. Monkeys and apes usually climb through trees. They use their arms and legs to walk. Sometimes, though, primates walk around on two legs. When they do, they look human-like. This is the case with a gorilla named Ambam.

Ambam lives in a zoo in the United Kingdom. The 21-year-old gorilla is huge. He weighs nearly 500 pounds (227 kg). Despite his large size, he looks like a person when he walks around on two legs. His unusual walking style has made him popular. One zookeeper said, "All gorillas can do it to some extent but we haven't got any who do it like Ambam . . . he is quite a celebrity at the park."

Zoo workers think they know why he walks around like this. They think he is trying to get a better view of food. He can see his keepers coming from farther away when he stands up. It also means Ambam can carry more food while moving around.

Ambam stands up just like a person!

5

The Bike-Riding Dog

Riding a scooter or a bike is a simple task for most people. But imagine seeing a big, shaggy dog cruising down the street on a bicycle. That's exactly what the neighbors of Norman the dog often see.

Norman lives in Canton, Georgia, with his owner Karen Cobb. She trained Norman to become a skilled bike and scooter rider. He even set a world record in 2013. He became the fastest dog to ever ride a scooter 98 feet (30 m). Norman zoomed across that distance in less than 21 seconds. He celebrated with a run around the gym where he set the record.

Bikes and scooters are not the only things Norman rides. He has also tried skateboarding and surfing. One person who watched Norman ride around was especially stunned: "It looks like a little man in a dog outfit."

FUN FACT
Norman is so talented he got his own television show. He appeared on the show with Tillman, a skateboarding dog.

Norman goes for a ride down the street.

Musical Dogs

A dog that could play the piano would be impressive. A dog jumping through hoops and riding on horseback would be amazing, too. And a dog that could ride a skateboard and jump rope would stun audiences. But what if a dog could do all those things? What if *two* dogs could do all those things?

Jacob and Jessica might be two of the most talented dogs on Earth. The Jack Russell terriers can do all of these tricks and more. Their trainer, Rachael Grylls, shows them off at dog shows. It took a year and a half to teach the dogs all these talents.

Some dogs can ride skateboards.

However, the training was not easy. Grylls spent almost an hour every day training the dogs. That was a lot for them. Jack Russell terriers lose focus quickly. Grylls said rewards make the training fun. "I just encourage them by making the tasks fun and rewarding them with bits of garlic sausage and lots of love."

Jacob and Jessica play the piano.

Jack the Balancing Dog

Jack lives in San Francisco, California, with his owner. Jack is an Australian cattle dog. This breed is known for helping lead cows on long journeys. But Jack has a special talent that is totally different. He is great at balancing things on his head.

Jack balances a teakettle on his head.

His owner, Nicole Lee, discovered the talent by accident. She said, "The balancing act started when we tried balancing a kernel of popcorn on his nose one night." She and her boyfriend noticed Jack was great at balancing. They wanted to see if Jack could balance other objects.

To their surprise, Jack could balance just about anything on his head. He was able to balance an egg and a clock. He could even balance a stack of coins. Lee started to train him. She cheered for him when he was able to balance a new item. "He responds really well to praise, so we use that as a reward."

FUN FACT
Lee's boyfriend asked people on the Internet for suggestions about things for Jack to balance. He got more than 1,000 responses. People suggested a can of soup, a glass of water, and many other things.

Halloween Dolphins

You have probably been trick-or-treating before. Every Halloween, millions of kids dress up in costumes. They go door-to-door in their neighborhoods. Their neighbors give them lots of candy. But imagine if kids got fish instead of candy. That was the treat two dolphins got for Halloween in 2008.

Sadie and Chelsea go trick-or-treating.

Sadie and Chelsea were two dolphins living at a marine park in California. They often performed for park visitors. The dolphins would leap into the air and play with toys. They followed their trainers' directions. For Halloween, a special show was planned.

FUN FACT
Dolphins love to eat fish. They can eat lots of them. An adult dolphin can eat up to 50 pounds (23 kg) of fish in one day!

One dolphin swam to the surface and held up a plastic jack-o'-lantern. The other showed off a spooky plastic skull. As a reward, the dolphins received some fresh **herring**! If you got a fish for Halloween, you might think it was a mean trick. But for the talented dolphins, it was a tasty treat.

Herring are a good treat for dolphins.

The Gorilla Artist

People love unique artwork. Some even buy artwork by kids to display in their homes. It is not that unusual to have a piece of art by a nine-year-old. But what if it is made by a nine-year-old gorilla?

N'Dowe the gorilla lives at a zoo in the United Kingdom. In 2013, zookeepers thought up an idea to raise money and have fun. First, they gave N'Dowe a gorilla statue a little bit smaller than himself. Then, they gave him a bunch of paint. He painted all over the statue. But he did not use brushes. Instead, he just used his fingers. As payment for his work, the zookeepers gave him grapes.

The painting was not just for fun. When N'Dowe was finished, zookeepers put the unique statue up for sale. As one zoo worker said, "This might be the first gorilla **sculpture** ever painted by a real live gorilla!" Zookeepers used the money to help protect wild gorillas.

Some animals can learn to paint.

N'Dowe paints his gorilla statue.

Sports Pigs

The racers lined up at the start line. They got ready to dive into the pool. Ready, set, go! They started swimming furiously. But they did not seem interested in finishing the race. Some even started bumping into one another. What was going on? The racers were not people. They were pigs!

Pigs get ready for a race in the pool.

The Sport-Pig **Federation** is a group that runs sporting events for pigs. The swimmers were at the federation's third annual contest. They competed in Moscow, Russia. Swimming was not the only event. Pigs also raced on foot. They played a game with a ball. Pigs from seven different countries came to the contest. They did not understand the events, of course. Their coaches had to follow behind them. They encouraged the pigs to run or swim.

One of the contest organizers said that the pigs will not end up on someone's dinner table. "How could you eat a competitor who is known around the world?"

Pigs are smart animals.

Squirrel on the Waves

Water-skiing can be a great way to spend a hot summer day. You can glide over the cool water behind a zooming **speedboat**. If you are waterskiing in Florida, do not be surprised if you see something unusual. A tiny, furry water-skier might zip past you. Her name is Twiggy the Water-skiing Squirrel.

Twiggy's owner, Lou Ann Best, has trained several squirrels to water-ski. All of them have been named Twiggy. Her husband, Chuck, found the first Twiggy in 1978. The young squirrel had become lost after a **hurricane**. The Bests adopted Twiggy. Chuck bought his daughter, Lalainia, a toy motor boat. Then, he had the idea to teach Twiggy how to water-ski.

The Bests' squirrels have been amazing audiences ever since. Twiggy rides on special plastic skis behind a toy boat. She even wears a tiny life vest. The squirrel has become so popular that she has been in movies.

Humans aren't the only living things that can water-ski.

Twiggy goes for a spin
on her water skis.

A Brainy Gorilla

Many people communicate using **sign language**. Rather than using their mouths, they talk with their hands. Different hand shapes stand for different words and ideas. Sign language is great for people who cannot hear. But could an animal be smart enough to learn it? That's the question Francine Patterson asked in the 1970s. She worked with a gorilla named Koko. Patterson wanted to teach Koko to sign.

The project was an amazing success. Over the next 40 years, Patterson has taught Koko about 1,000 different signs. She also taught the gorilla to understand more than 2,000 spoken words. Koko's intelligence and language learning have shocked scientists. She even combines signs to make new words. When she saw a ring, she used the signs for "finger" and "bracelet."

Koko even keeps pets. She loves kittens. She has cared for several different cats over the years. Koko also paints pictures. She names the paintings using signs. Koko's intelligence and personality have changed many people's view of gorillas.

Patterson teaches a young
Koko how to sign.

federation (fed-uh-RAY-shun) A federation is a group in charge of something. The Sport-Pig Federation runs pig sporting events.

herring (HER-ing) Herring are fish that live in northern seas. Dolphins Sadie and Chelsea got to eat herring as a reward.

hurricane (HUR-uh-kayn) A hurricane is a large, powerful storm with swirling winds. Twiggy the squirrel got lost in a hurricane.

primates (PRY-maytz) Primates are types of mammals that include apes, monkeys, and humans. People and gorillas are kinds of primates.

sculpture (SKULPT-chur) A sculpture is a piece of artwork that is molded or carved. N'Dowe the gorilla painted a sculpture.

sign language (sine LANG-wij) Sign language is a way for people to talk with each other using their hands. Koko the gorilla learned a special kind of sign language.

speedboat (SPEED-boht) A speedboat is a boat with a powerful motor. Twiggy the squirrel can water-ski behind a tiny speedboat.

BOOKS

125 True Stories of Amazing Animals: Inspiring Tales of Animal Friendship and Four-Legged Heroes, Plus Crazy Animal Antics. Washington, DC: National Geographic, 2012.

Haggerty, Babette. *The Best Dog Tricks on the Planet: 125 Amazing Things Your Dog Can Do on Command.* Salem, MA: Page Street, 2013.

Newman, Aline Alexander. *Animal Superstars: And More True Stories of Amazing Animal Talents.* Washington, DC: National Geographic, 2013.

WEB SITES

Visit our Web site for links about animal tricks and talents: *childsworld.com/links*

Note to Parents, Teachers, and Librarians:
We routinely verify our Web links to make sure they are safe and active sites. So encourage your readers to check them out!

INDEX